THE SMART MONEY METHOD

A BETTER WAY
TO SAVE, PROTECT, AND GROW
YOUR RETIREMENT NEST EGG
(TAX FREE)

RICHARD HOLTHEUER

The Smart Money Method:
A Better Way to Save, Protect, and Grow
Your Retirement Nest Egg (Tax Free)

Copyright © 2017, 2020 by Richard Holtheuer

All Rights Reserved. Without limiting the rights under the copyright reserved above, this book may not be reproduced, in whole or in part, stored in a retrieval system, or transmitted in any form or by any means (electronic, mechanical, photocopying, recording, or otherwise) except for brief quotations in critical reviews or publications without the prior permission of the author.

Limit of Liability: Although the author has made every reasonable attempt to achieve complete accuracy of the content in this book, he makes no representations or warranties with respect to the accuracy or completeness of the contents of this book. Your unique circumstances may not be suited to the examples illustrated in this book. This book is not intended to replace professional legal or financial advice for your specific situation, and you should always seek the advice of licensed professionals.

ISBN: 979-8-6177-3273-5

Table of Contents

- Why Listen to Me? 1
- Why Consider My Solutions? 7
- What You Will Learn Here 9

- ▷ ...What's Wrong with My 401(k)? 11
  - Some People Kept It All 17
  - The Little-Known Alternative 21
  - How It Works 23
  - Safety of Insurance Carriers Underwriting IULs 25
  - Historic Retirement Saving 27

- ▷ Why They Are Outmoded 29
  - Risk 31
  - Taxes 33
  - Management Fees 37
  - Death Tax for Your Heirs 43
  - Longevity Risk 45

- ▷ Circle Back to the IULs 47
  - Loans—More about Borrowing from Yourself 53
  - The All-Important 'Living Benefits' 57
  - Truly Safe 59
  - Information—When You Act on It—Is Power 61

- ▷ Is It Too Late to Start Funding an IUL? 63
  - Can I Afford to Do This? 67
  - Run the Numbers 69
  - Learn More 73

My Disclaimer

THE INFORMATION SHARED IN THIS book is intended to provide general knowledge about current tax advantages and risk-free strategies within insurance policies, annuity products, and other asset management vehicles. It is not, however, intended to provide specific legal or tax advice.

Examples of strategies and outcomes obtained by real people are mentioned in the book, but they do not provide any guarantees of your own returns. Recommendations for using the solutions within the book are reserved to state-specific licensed insurance, tax, and financial professionals.

The strategies discussed within the book cannot be used to avoid IRS penalties or appropriate taxes. The book does not promote specific equity market investments, insurance companies, or financial institutions. It is not meant to recommend any specific individual tax plan or arrangement. You are encouraged to consult your, CPA, tax attorney or retirement adviser regarding any of the concepts discussed herein.

Product guarantees are backed by the financial strength and claims-paying ability of the issuing insurer, not by the insurance agent or financial adviser.

Product and features availability may vary from State to State.

For full details on how life insurance and annuities perform, including expenses and costs of insurance inquire through our website: www.holtheuergroup.com

Dedication

THIS BOOK IS DEDICATED TO you who are hard-working moms, dads and entrepreneurs who go out every day into the world to produce for your families and work hard to provide and secure a piece of the American Dream.

I have been meeting with you for many years. I have been listening to all your worries and concerns. Money is not everything (if you asked me), but it sure helps to make life easier. You make it, you spend it and invest some of it. In the end it will be whatever you get to keep after taxes, fees and market moves.

I have make it my job to help you keep the most money possible and to protect it once you have it, so you can have that well-deserved vacation after hard work, paying off the mortgage, putting kids through school—and the job changes and changes that just come with living life.

Life is never a straight line, there will be curves, obstacles and challenges, and the last thing you want to worry about is whether you will have enough money to do whatever it is that you want to do after your working years.

It is for this very reason that I decided to write this book. I know that the strategy I share with you is completely new to you. Don't worry about that: Up until now, only the wealthy with their access to top notch (and expensive) advisers have been benefitting from this system. Yet anyone who pays attention and takes the time to learn and implement it with the right IUL trained advisor can and will benefit from it.

If you already know about this vehicle for retirement wealth, congratulations! You are using the most powerful strategy available in the tax code today. However, it's been my experience that 9 out of 10 people have never heard of it—their advisor or CPA never brought it up because they just didn't know about it.

 Why Listen to Me?

I BEGAN MY CAREER BACK in 1989 when Life Insurance was sold door to door and we collected the insurance premiums in cash. It was called debit insurance. I was responsible for collecting a $6,400-a-month book and offering whole life policies to people in the neighborhood. The areas I worked were a little rough, crime was an issue and I had to be mindful of where I was at any given time.

Then, in 1990 I received a postcard from an agency in downtown Miami looking for an agent to work ordinary insurance for Mutual of Omaha, a well-respected and well-known insurance carrier which is a household name today. That is when my education in this great field of finance began.

It was there, with Mutual of Omaha, that I also had my first life insurance claim. I will never forget it. I had been in contact this young lady for about 6 months to sell her a Universal Life Insurance for $100,000 coverage. She was interested in it but had no time to meet with me. Her mother was already a client at the time and so she helped me finally get the meeting. We applied for the coverage and the daughter was approved as applied. She was getting married that year. Indeed, her fiancé and I were planning on getting together to go over his policy as well.

It had been about three months since she had become my client when I received a call from her mom. She was very upset, and she proceeded to tell me that her daughter was no longer with us. It was like a bucket of frozen water had been poured on me. I was in disbelief. Deceased? I knew this young lady. She was so full of life and happy planning for her wedding. As it happens, her death was reported in the news media. There had been a home invasion that went bad. She was fatally wounded and died.

The insurance company paid the claim and I delivered it to her mom in person. It was at that moment that I first realized the implications of my job, my career. I thought of the moment she agreed to finally meet with me. I thought of the time I had spent chasing her to buy. I realized then that she probably never really thought seriously of death (and certainly not her own) and that she may have agreed because of her mom and my persistence.

Nobody thinks they are going to die any time soon, certainly not when they are a healthy 27-year-old.

My life changed that day. I became more aware of our mortality. Thought more about how this affects those around us. More aware of my role in people's life and responsibility. My eyes were opened.

Eventually I became independent and obtained my series 6 and 65 licenses as an investment adviser and my RIA (Registered Investment Advisor status). For the past 30 years I have not been on the payroll of any company, but only paid through commissions (1099 income, as my accountant would say).

I would not do anything else. I love what I do even though the road has been a bit rocky at times.

Story of a Funded Illness

I would like here and now to give you a sneak peek at just one of the benefits of the right alternative instrument for saving and growing your hard-earned cash.

Recently a good friend of mine as well as my client (I'll call him Jack) suffered a heart attack. He survived but Jack was flat on his back on extended sick leave from work. He was healing; he wasn't earning.

Luckily, we had started his 'new investment plan' a mere two years earlier. As he held an IUL, he was able to receive (almost immediately, in fact) a directly deposited cash amount of $800,000 into his bank account. Why? The IUL offers 'living benefits' that fund critical illness claims. Since a heart attack can definitely be called 'critical', his claim was approved and processed right away.

And by the way, as it sometimes happens, his wife thought it was a bad idea at the time to invest in an Indexed Universal Life insurance policy! She changed her mind quickly when she recognized that she and Jack had virtually no time to worry about where the money would come from to pay his out-of-pocket medical expenses and their monthly bills (mortgage payments, and so on).

I'll be talking in these pages about that IUL that Jack subscribed to, and why you should do so too. I'll be keeping in mind all the objections and protestations his wife had so that I can provide you with the answers I gave her and Jack.

My clients become my friends. My friends become clients. I do not see much of a distinction between the two. If you care about someone, you will do everything you can to protect them, to help them grow in their life, to make sure that their loved ones will be cared for as well.

I have learned what I know because of the many people I have had the opportunity to work with. I have been successful in my career because of the success of my clients and the referrals they bring. I believe that when you take the long road, you put your client first and do more than you promised, your blessings multiply.

I have seen many agents and advisors come and go. It is not an easy business to start nor to keep going. I trained eight agents when I was with Mutual of Omaha and only one remains active in the business today.

I have been asked what makes my agency different from the rest and how I differentiate myself from competition. I believe that I am my biggest competitor. I strive to be better than yesterday and to learn more about how to improve my client's financial security and success. In that sense, I really do not have any higher competition. My desire to serve and to educate my friends/clients is what separates me from the pack. It is simply an attitude.

It is true that if you want to have a reward, you must take some risk, but . . .

 # Why Consider My Solutions?

YOU TAKE RISKS AND MAKE sacrifices to invest so that someday you will enjoy financial security—freedom from worries about money. The goal for everyone who works for a living is to have enough money to independently and comfortably retire and potentially to leave a legacy to loved ones.

In my 29 years working as an independent advisor, I have heard many horror stories about how much money was lost in various stock market crashes (there will always be numerous dips in the markets during one's lifetime), bad real estate investments and hot stock tips a neighbor recommended. If you have not yet experienced any of these, you surely know someone who has.

It is true that if you want to have a reward, you must take some risk. Hopefully you have had the facts to calculate that risk, but if your neighbor the plumber is recommending that hot stock, there probably aren't many facts to back up the recommendation. That bad real estate investment was too good to be true because no seriously informed professional investor wanted to risk his money in such a bad neighborhood. If facts are scarce, we should run from the investment. We don't always.

I would like you to know that there are other paths to wealth that have none of the risks associated with the traditional or mainstream retirement or investment plans available today. The information in these pages will help you understand that you have choices and allow you to make better decisions on where to save/invest for retirement or for profit, so you may enjoy a better financial future and peace of mind.

What You Will Learn Here

YOU WILL LEARN A NEW strategy that has been used mainly by the very wealthy and savvy investors since it was introduced by Congress and the IRS back in the early 1980s. It is not only more of a 'safe-haven' for your hard-earned cash than mainstream instruments but can be implemented by anyone who is saving for retirement. Using this instrument, you will be better prepared to ride out the next market crash (principle intact), have an exit strategy for your retirement (with tax advantages), and a tax-exempt income that can last for a long as you live.

I will be calling it a tool, a vehicle, an instrument, a plan and a policy—and it is all this! That is how well designed this is and how powerful it is in protecting your saved cash and growing it through interest paid and profits earned (on the investments the cash is put into).

Saving for retirement is one of those things in life that unfortunately does not offer second chances. If you do not like what you find (mainstream investment instruments like the 401(k) and others) you must take a different road. A successful plan must have these four legs to stand on.

It must:

 1. be based on time-tested investment history
 2. have a plan for the next market crash
 3. have an exit strategy
 4. be self-completing

As we progress through this information, it will become more and more evident that your current retirement plan does not stand on any of these legs! I know this for a fact, because unfortunately you are probably saving in one of these mainstream plans:

- 401(k)
- IRA
- SEP
- 403(b)
- Roth IRA

It is not your fault; these are what it is offered by your employer or pushed by your CPA if you own a business. There are other options and just because your company or CPA has not heard of them does not mean they are not legal, time-tested, tax-advantaged and easy to subscribe to. And they are not reserved for the wealthy! Far from it as we will be seeing.

...What's Wrong with My 401(k)?

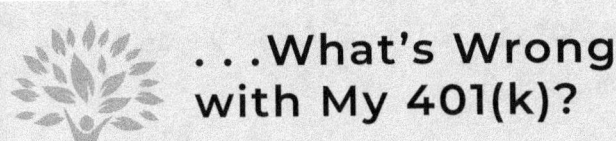

I DON'T WANT TO FRIGHTEN you if you hold a 401(k) or any of the instruments I listed above.

However, there is the problem with a 401(k) and similar products, and those of you old enough to have lived the 2007 market crash know what it is right now: They invest in stocks, bonds and other instruments offered on the stock exchanges. Stock markets are by definition and history volatile places to hold your money. When the stock market crashes (a term for an abrupt and deep decline in stock prices across the whole market), the dollar value of your 401(k) also plummets.

If you had a million dollars to retire in 2007 and you were planning to call it quits and retire in 2008, you would have had about $530,000 left after that year's market crash. That end number does not take into consideration the income taxes and the management fees you'd have to pay on top of it. Those individuals who wanted to retire in 2008, 2009 and after could not do it. They could not do it because the market had not risen enough for their accounts to go back up to their pre-2007 values. It took almost 9 years to get back to break even.

Those investors did everything right according to traditional investing rules. However, what the market giveth it taketh away (and it did, big time in 2007, 2008 and for a while thereafter).

I have met with many of these folks who lost a big chunk of their financial life on that crash. It is not an easy conversation; some got physically sick at the news and never recovered. Some resigned themselves to living off a meager Social Security benefit. It didn't feel good for a long time for millions of Americans.

What assurance do you have that your plan will not suffer such a fate? When will the next crash happen? And how many more will you experience before you need your money? These are tough questions to answer, but it is better to ask now and have a plan today for whatever tomorrow may bring.

What's sad about such market ups and downs is that you do not know who to ask for accountability. Who failed? Was it the government? The adviser? The system? Where do you go for answers? The cruel reality is that when you own one of these type of retirement plans—linked to the money markets (aka stock exchanges) you are on your own. You assume all the risk and you pay all the fees and taxes...hoping enough is left to pay your costs of living.

History tends to repeat itself, and humans tend to forget that it does. When will the next crash happen? On the chart at the end of this section, we can see the last 10 market crashes that we experienced. The image starts with 1901 (our grandparents' or great grandparents' era) through the more familiar 'Dot Com' crash that this millennium welcomed and ends with the so-called 'Mortgage and Financial Crash' that reared its head starting in 2007.

The average loss in most of those crashes was 47%. Look at the dates and you'll see that the crashes occurred at an average of 11-year intervals—with a couple of events happening right on the heels of the prior one!

Don't feel frightened. Just be determined to learn this financial history lesson! We need to accept that it is only a matter of time before we see another stock market crash. We need to develop a strategy to avoid the losses it will bring—by having a 'safe-haven' strategy in place.

Most people don't learn this history. Thus, even after the poor performance of all 401(k) accounts (and indeed all stock-invested trading accounts) in the last market crash people continued to fund them. I guess they just think, "C'est la vie—That's life." They desperately or blindly hope that this time it will be different.

What is surprising to me is that when I ask if they know which specific investments are part of their 401(k) portfolio, almost 90% do not know. What is worse, they do not even understand how the investments work, are decided and how much they (should) return in profits. It is a form of gambling: You put money in. If the market goes up, you win. If you were wrong, you lose.

It is important to note here that the investment companies will get their fees either way. You lose, they win. You win, they win. The risk is all on you. So, how in the world can you win with all the odds stacked against you? Can you afford to lose 30-50% of your hard-earned money the next time the bubble bursts?

After the market crashes of 2000 and 2007 some people began to wonder whether saving for retirement in a 401(k) or IRA was indeed a good idea. They get that markets go up and down, but the extent of the losses in the last crash averaged 47%—about half of people's account value disappeared. That was finally enough to jolt some people to an awake state. It made more people aware that market losses are real, and they can be devastating to a financial future.

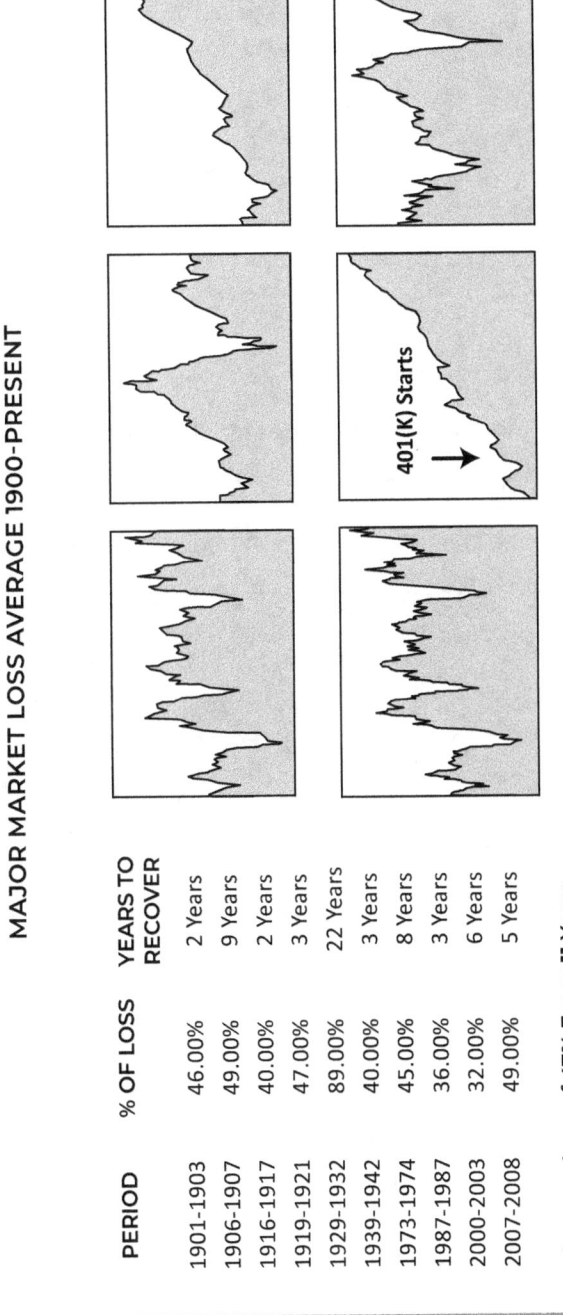

What you may not know is that some people who are saving for retirement did not lose a single penny when that last (or any prior) crash took place.

Some People Kept It All

LET ME GO BACK TO my comment about having a safe-haven strategy for your hard-earned money. What I mean by that is that you must find and learn (in these pages, in fact) about the vehicles that can

- ✓ 1. Protect your principle from being decimated
- ✓ 2. Earn profits based on the performance of an Index outside of the market
- ✓ 3. Earn interest with double digit potential and a zero floor (zero is your hero)
- ✓ 4. Protect the earned profits and interest with a yearly lock and reset

What you may not know is that some people who are saving for retirement did not lose a single penny when that last (or any prior) crash took place. Their accounts have grown steadily—just as I described in the four points above—even with the stock market volatility we now experience on a day to day basis.

What they did was to simply invest in a plan that is not subject to market losses. They are using plans that have been historically subscribed to mainly by the wealthy. The good news is that anyone—of any net worth—can benefit from this strategy today. The only difference will be the number of zeroes to the right of the account balance.

I know what you are thinking. A plan that does not lose any money? You read me correctly! You sit on the sideline when the market is going down. When the market or index goes up, you capture returns up to a cap. This 'cap' is built into these instruments, so it protects your money and past earned profits automatically. You never have to 'recover' from negative or 'crash' years with these vehicles.

Story of a Safe Haven Strategy that Built Abundance

Alex came to me shortly after the market crash of 2007. Alex was 44 when we first started working together. He wanted to know if there was any way to protect his money from any future crashes.

Why come with such a question? Easy: He had just lost about $135,000 of his hard-earned money from his 401(k) due to the plummeting stock market.

I spent some time educating him on the alternative that might best suit him. He opened an IUL—Indexed Universal Life insurance policy—with a $500/month contribution.

He is projected to get about $46,000/year tax-free starting at age 65, for the rest of his life—$46,000 every year without fail until his death.

He is single and has moved other assets into a second IUL that is projected to provide him with another $35,000 tax-free dollars every year for the rest of his life. $81,000 per year is a nice cushy retirement!

The projections we used were based on a 6.5% compounded annual rate of return (actual gain after fees and expenses). His actual return has been a little better than projected to date.

I have reminded him that his IUL also provides living benefits in the event of a critical Illness, chronic Illness, critical injury and terminal illness—like I did for Jack and his spouse. All these benefits are tax-free.

Only about 10% of the wealthiest Americans invest in an alternative, safe-haven plan such as the one I'm presenting here, and already own 55% of all the assets invested.

 # The Little-Known Alternative

MOST SAVERS INVEST THEIR MONEY in a 401, IRA or Roth IRA because that is what they have 'easy access' to. However, the last crash showed us that market-invested instruments can be decimated overnight.

Only about 10% of the wealthiest Americans invest in an alternative, safe-haven plan such as the one I'm presenting here, and already own 55% of all the assets invested. They own this large share of the assets for a simple reason: The wealthy, through their high-priced advisors, are virtually the only ones who have known about this alternative—and I am trying to change that for your benefit!

This alternative, safe-haven plan is a tax-free alternative that uses a little-known code IRC 7702 (per Investopedia. com, *"Section 7702 of the U.S. Internal Revenue Code defines what the federal government considers to be a legitimate life insurance contract and determines how such contracts are to be taxed. It applies to life insurance contracts issued after 1985."*).

Most people do not know about this alternative. In fact, many CPAs and other finance industry professionals I have talked to do not know about it or use it for their clients' wealth planning. You would assume that a legal instrument with such advantages as this one offers would be common knowledge in the industry, but it is not. This type of planning requires special training and not all financial advisers have acquired the skill.

So, if you are planning on going to your accountant or CPA to get advice about this instrument, you most likely will not get any answers. It is not their fault. They do not have to look for ways to protect your money! Their main job is to file your tax returns and save you money with some basic tax planning and bookkeeping.

How It Works

THESE EQUITY-INDEXED UNIVERSAL LIFE INSURANCE policies, or IULs, are set up in a way to use the minimum amount of insurance for a maximum cash value accumulation. Yes, they are life insurance, and fully act as life insurance policies—but they are in fact supercharged to <u>*also*</u> grow your money for retirement.

You subscribe to a life insurance policy of the specific type described in 1985 by the above-cited law. You grow your cash value tax deferred. You take retirement income <u>tax-free</u> through <u>tax-free</u> loans collateralized by the cash value of the policy. You are taking a loan from yourself—from your own policy—and not a withdrawal or a 'surrendered' amount as is done from 401(k) accounts and the like. By taking a loan instead of making a straight withdrawal from your policy, the main benefit of this strategy—tax free cash—is preserved (again, according to the design of this instrument and described in the above law).

In the last market crash, we had 457 banks and financial investment companies go belly up. Only 2 (two!) insurance companies got into financial trouble and one of them got bailed out.

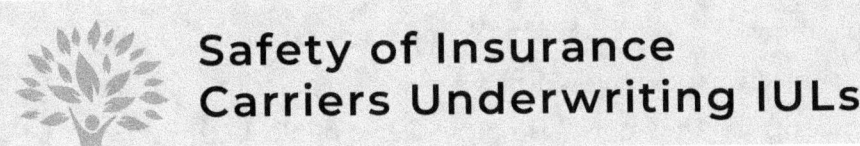

Safety of Insurance Carriers Underwriting IULs

NOW HERE IS A QUESTION I get asked a lot: What happens if the insurance company underwriting this IUL goes belly up?

In the last market crash, we had 457 banks and financial investment companies go belly up. Only 2 (two!) insurance companies got into financial trouble and one of them got bailed out. This information is public. And it is good news: If you are doing business with an established (i.e. one that has been around for over a century—as many have been) insurance carrier there should be no problem and your money is safe. We only work with A+ or higher rated institutions, and world renown carriers generally all over 150 years old.

The insurance companies are the most resilient financial institutions today. They are heavily regulated and cannot speculate with the money they manage for other people. As an industry, there are fewer failures than any other sector.

When they invest in variable products or market-related type of investments, they must set up a separate account and are subjected to a whole different set of regulations, audits and controls. They must also provide the public with information on the risk associated with the investments, the guarantees provided and a prospectus—just as you do when you buy a Mutual Fund.

Historic Retirement Saving

THE WAY WE HAVE SAVED for retirement till now was not created in one law in one year but evolved over a large portion of the 20th century. And here we are in 2020, and the whole system is now outmoded—in fact, many professionals around me are saying that it is ripe to implode on itself.

For most of the last 50-75 years, people saved in one or more of these three types of saving plans:

- ✅ 1. A qualified plan, such as a 401(k), IRA, 403(b) or a Roth IRA.
- ✅ 2. A defined benefit plan. The defined benefit plan of the 20th century has been disappearing. The new options are loaded with penalties, market risk and high fees.
- ✅ 3. A nonqualified type of plan such as money in the market, stocks, real estate ownership, private pensions, cash value life insurance (not IULs) and annuities.

Three other reasons clearly show that these 20th century retirement savings plans are not made for us in the 21st century . . .

1) Risks
2) Taxes
3) Management fees

Why They Are Outmoded

I'VE ALREADY MENTIONED THE SCARY market crashes (aka recessions, when the stock markets take a dramatic dive and reduce our portfolio values to a fraction of what they used to be).

Three other reasons clearly show that these 20th century retirement savings plans are not made for us in the 21st century. Those three reasons are:

- Risks
- Taxes
- Management fees

The existence of these three factors means that any traditional 20th century vehicle you subscribe to for retirement will not earn as much as it could if it were designed—not for the IRS or your stockbroker—but for your own real wealth creation and preservation.

> "You put up 100% of your capital, take 100% of the risk to get maybe 30% of the return."
>
> — Mr. Jack Bogle, former CEO of Vanguard

 # Risk

ONE OF THE PROBLEMS THAT qualified plans presented is that the owners became the person responsible for the selection of the underlying investments, making him or her practically the money manager. The risk of the performance of these types of accounts was also transferred to the individual or employee.

Mr. Jack Bogle, former CEO of Vanguard the pioneer of indexed funds, referring to the investor in 401(k)s, once said, "You put up 100% of your capital, take 100% of the risk to get maybe 30% of the return".

There is no need—once you've created this alternative investment vehicle—to take 100% of the risks for a shoddy return.

New additional taxes (surtaxes and others that sneak in to decimate our wealth) are created every couple of years without us realizing it.

Taxes

IF YOU HAPPEN TO BE a wise investor and manage to get a decent return by selecting good investments and building a large account, then you must deal with the possibility of taxes being higher when you retire and need to withdraw the money than they are today.

I could go on and on about how taxes never go down, and that new additional taxes (surtaxes and others that sneak in to decimate our wealth) are created every couple of years without us realizing it.

Why? Well, if we look at our situation, such as the national debt, deficit and unfunded liabilities (Medicare, Social Security, Medicaid and VA programs just to name a few of the hundreds of taxpayer funded programs the Federal and State governments run) together with the growing number of folks retiring today (1000 per day), it is impossible to expect taxes to remain the same. Thus, unknown amounts of taxes become one of the biggest risks associated with these plans.

By looking at the chart on the next page—particularly the black bars representing the interest that we are piling up as a percentage of GDP—it becomes hard to imagine that taxes would ever decrease.

Our GDP or gross domestic product is the wealth that we as a nation create. It is not the amount of taxes we pay in but the taxable amounts of money the nation earns in a collective manner. The left chart's black horizontal line shows the affordability of our social welfare and retirement programs slipping through our collective fingers, as their cost rises far above the GDP that supports them.

In the right chart we see that—although taxes were high between the Depression years and the mid-1970s—the taxes we collectively pay in has decreased and settled pretty much at their all-time low. This means that the government should not be able to pay for the programs they are paying for!

How long can this last? If we heads of household ran our home earnings/spending like this, we'd individually be so deep in debt that we are ready for the proverbial Debtor's Prison!

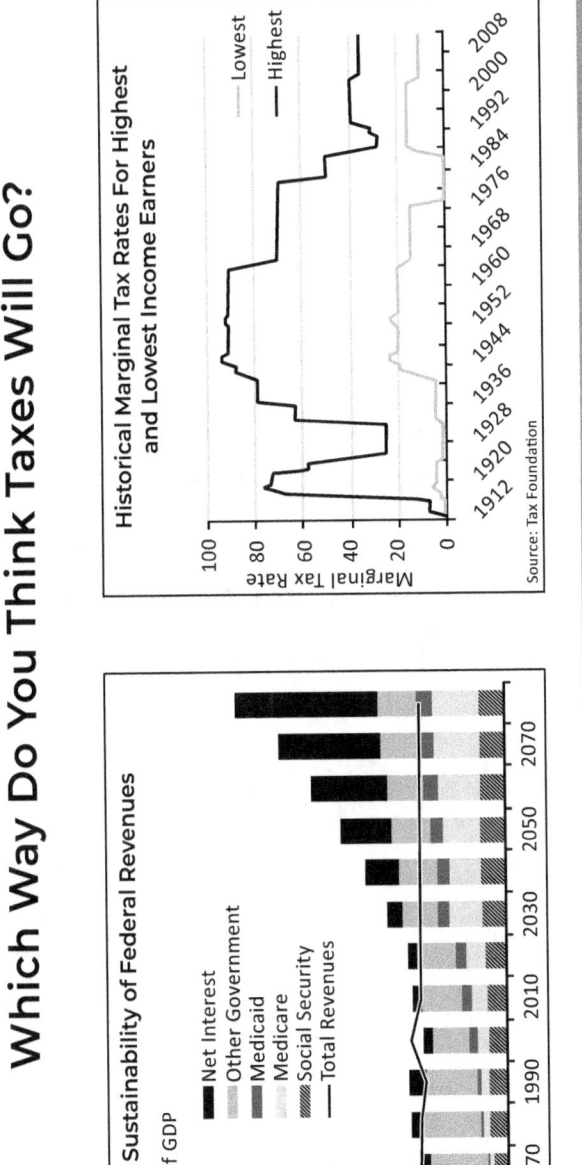

The sad fact is that most people have absolutely no clue how much money they're paying other people out of their 401(k) accounts.

Management Fees

THERE ARE TWO SETS OF fees that these 20th century savings/retirement plans have, yet most people do not know what they are or how they will affect the growth of the investment over a lifetime.

Thus, the third overlooked and misunderstood risk is the management fees that must be paid on each account for someone to 'manage' it for you, and fees on each transaction you undertake in such accounts.

Most people are not aware that there are 2 sets of fees coming out of their traditional retirement accounts, be it their 401(k) or their investments within those accounts.

Mutual funds are often a selection within a 401(k) account, alongside 'regular' stocks. A Forbes study shows that the average cost for a Mutual Fund across the US is 4.17%. You also have the administrative ('management') fee which is between 0.5 to 1.5% depending on the size of the employer. Your total cost is the sum of these two or a potential 5.67%.

These recurring fees can reduce the account balance by 30-50% over a lifetime. It is an expensive part of the equation as you can see.

The sad fact is that most people have absolutely no clue how much money they're paying other people out of their 401(k) accounts. Why it is so important to know this? Well, the difference between someone paying 1% and another paying 2% for the same services and plan can mean that the second person runs out of money 10 years sooner than the first one! Considering that 2% fees run annually for over 30 or 40 years, you stand to lose about half of the money in your account to Wall Street advisers, plan administrators and stock brokerages. Sadly, these fees are charged whether your account is growing or losing money.

Do you have any idea how much you pay for (and lose from) your retirement accounts? After all, you probably know the interest rate you pay for your home mortgage and car loan, right? It would make sense to know how much you pay for 401(k), IRA, pensions and other related types of plan.

Are you beginning to realize what 'theft' goes on in your retirement plan? I hope that you can take the time to check how much you are paying for your retirement plan. If not, you may be in for a rude surprise at the end of your working career.

For most, the retirement account will be the biggest asset they own. If the manager or investment administrator won't tell you clearly how much they charge, shop elsewhere.

Story of a 401(k)

Lynn was a client of mine. She was laid off after 7 years of employment at a marketing company. She held a 401(k) and called me to ask for advice. Why me? She also held an IUL that we had set up together some time before.

Her dilemma was this: She was going to liquidate part of her 401(k) to help pay the bills she was accumulating. If she did borrow from her 401(k), she would be hit with a 10% penalty for withdrawing before age 59 ½. She would also have to begin a repayment plan immediately and continue repayments for 5 years at the imposed interest rate (which was high). If she was laid off in the process of repaying her withdrawal from her 401(k), the money would be due in full within 90 days! Talk about being kicked while you are down!

I told Lynn to instead use the tax-free loan from her IUL. There would be no penalties. The interest rate was going to be well below market rate and certainly lower than the one imposed by the 401(k). She additionally could decide for herself when (and even if) she'd start to repay her IUL loan.

She took this path. Lynn was able to get the money she needed at 4.4% interest while her principal held in the IUL that year earned 5.5%. That provided a 1.1% positive arbitrage (more money gains to Lynn).

She will repay the funds into her policy soon. If she changes her mind and does not pay herself back, no problem: The loan will be liquidated at her death by the life insurance.

How to Figure Out Your 401(k) Expenses/Fees

Step 1: Tally Administrative Costs

- Go to your plan's summary annual report. Find the "basic financial statement" section.
- Subtract "benefits paid" from "total plan expenses."
- Divide that number by the total value of the plan.

- This number is your plan's administrative cost.

STEP 2: Calculate Investment Fees

- Multiply your fund expense ratio by your balance in the fund.
- Divide those total fees by your total balance.
- This number is your investment expense.

If you have only one fund (i.e. target-date fund), your investment expense ratio is the ratio on this one fund.

STEP 3: Add Administrative and Investment Fees for a grand total.

If you pass away holding an IUL, the money in it goes to the spouse or heirs *tax-free* (all of it—every last cent).

# Death Tax for Your Heirs

THERE IS ANOTHER BIG PROBLEM associated with the qualified retirement plans of the 20th century and I need to mention it here, even though it doesn't affect you, the investor, in a direct and personal way. It only affects you if you want to leave a legacy to heirs.

Let's say you do not 'make it' to your retirement date but die earlier. During your working and investing years, though, you built a sizeable account of cash. You pass away and the entire 401(k) is left to your heirs.

You have unknowingly created a tax bomb for them!

When a 401(k) owner dies, the account balance is typically paid in a lump sum and treated as income to the named beneficiaries (heirs). This bumps up those heirs' income for that year to the highest tax bracket and it wipes out in some cases up to 70% of the money supposedly inherited between Federal and State taxes.

Imagine, for instance, that you have $500,000 in your retirement plan and your heirs earn a taxable (AGI) $100,000 a year. In the year of your death, they would have to report $600,000 as taxable income—putting them at the top of their tax bracket!

This does not have to be your heirs' case when you invest in this alternative, tax-advantaged instrument. When you pass away holding an IUL, the money in it goes to the spouse or heirs tax-free (all of it—every last cent)—and whatever income they have earned in the same tax year is just taxed as it might have been without this inheritance.

Longevity Risk

IF YOU WANT TO KNOW the biggest and often best reason for getting into one of these policies, it is the fear associated with this question: "Will I outlive my retirement income?"

With the greater health that Baby Boomers (and even their parents who are our Centenarians today) enjoy, this is a big worry! How many Boomers will live to be Centenarians and beyond?

When comparing with our financial calculator the effect of taking money out of a qualified plan, then losing that principle plus potential interest (versus the tax-free safe-haven alternative), most accounts would be depleted after 5 to 7 years into retirement.

Why?

Because of the spiral effect that liquidating securities to generate income will do to the balance. Most people find themselves in a tough spot trying to determine how much money or percentage to take out in retirement from their qualified plan so that the money lasts for at least 20 to 25 years! This is stressful and leads to many disappointments. Usually, you are told to take no more than 4% so the funds will last. There is no guarantee that this—or any other formula someone else provides—will work.

Circle Back to the IULs

A PROPERLY STRUCTURED RETIREMENT PLAN needs to guarantee income way into age 90 or 100. How about income beyond 100? What your CPA or adviser may not know can hurt you. We are living longer and therefore need income for more time than our grandparents did just 30-40 years ago.

When properly structured and assuming conservative returns of say 6.5% with a 10% cap including all fees, the projected income can run to age 100. How much have these IUL's actual return been? Historically, about 8-9% for the last 25 years.

Investing some time in learning how to mitigate taxes and grow your investments will be time well spent. For every year that you wait to start with an IUL you lose about $5,000 per year in spendable income. Time is money, and you should take charge of your future now.

So, what is there to do to eliminate all these risk factors and not only protect the cash you have saved but protect the increase it brings you through interest and profits?

The picture below shows how the interest and earnings in an IUL are credited—and protected. You earn the profits and interest as the market booms and rises in value, yet when that same market busts or goes down in value you have built in protection of the earlier earnings and built in protection against further losses.

After seeing this why would anyone put money in a place where it will be taxed, need to pay out excessive fees and risk losing it—all of it!—in the next financial crash?

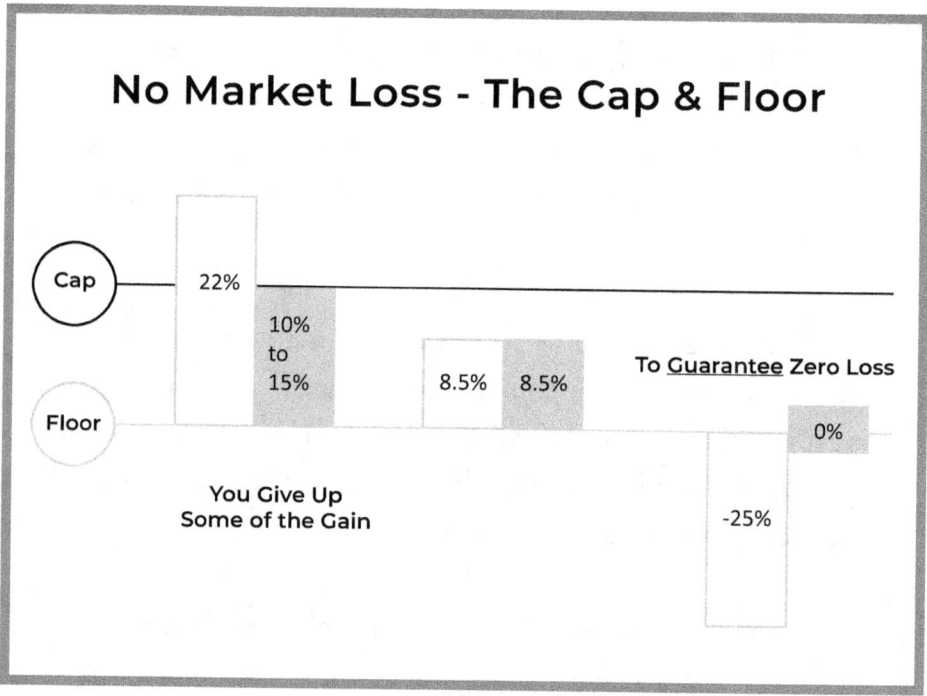

What we do to benefit from this life-long investment protection and growth is return to the strategy of subscribing to an _Equity Indexed Universal Life Insurance Policy_ (IUL) as your chief funding vehicle.

The original 1980s laws are the building blocks of this tax-free alternative retirement plan: The policy you build out needs to comply with Rule 7702 of the IRS code, that is true. A properly design IUL (Indexed Universal Life) Insurance Policy provides tax-free growth, tax-free distributions (now, or later for retirement) and protection from the decimation all-too common in the open stock market.

I cannot repeat this often enough: The IUL protects your money from the next market crashes.

The policy earns participation interest rates based on an outside index such as the S&P 500 or NASDAQ, affording participation in the open stock market's growth (with a cap) but downside protection when the market goes down. It eliminates future tax rate increases risk from your retirement plan. It allows for unlimited contributions and liquidity.

On the next chart below, you can see the beneficial effect a floor and a cap can have over time on your accumulation and growth of your retirement account.

The markets will always, always go up and down, up and down. Sometimes an industry or an individual stock will stay stable (its chart will show a horizontal line.) This is the way of the markets. This up and down volatility is what makes the average (and even professional) investor pull out his hair with fear and salivate with greed!

This upward market movement benefits you and means that your principle (the actual amount of cash you hold in the plan) grows steadily over time. When the market goes up, you capture positive returns.

When the market is in a downward swing, you go sideways instead of down like everyone else! For your investment (and the growth it has earned), there are no losses!

This protective strategy is automated, so you can rest assured that your money is safe—year after year and decade after decade that you hold the policy.

THE SMART MONEY METHOD

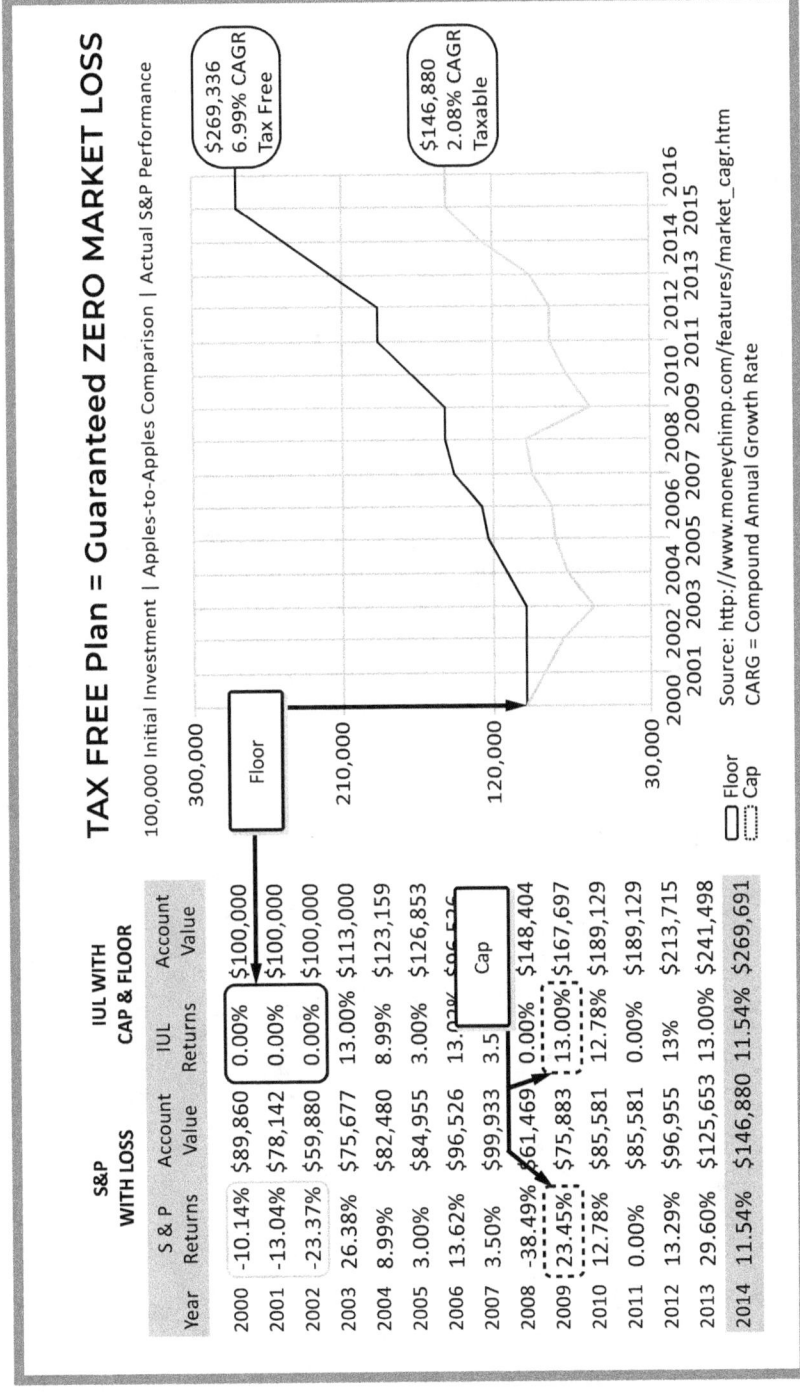

You can stop taking out loans from your local bank for your larger purchase needs.

Loans—More about Borrowing from Yourself

WHEN YOU HOLD THIS ALTERNATIVE, safe-haven instrument, you have a benefit virtually unknown to most retirement savers: You can stop taking out loans from your local bank for your larger purchase needs.

Story about a Loan Qualification

Jose had been a client for 17 years, funding his IUL for all those years. He was an entrepreneur and needed a loan to buy a van for his business.

Why did he call me? He called me because the bank his company did business with would not approve him for a $15,000 vehicle loan. He remembered what I had told him when educating him about the benefits of his IUL policy. Maybe he didn't need the bank after all.

And he was right! I told him that he could use the funds from his IUL (Indexed Universal Life) policy. His policy cash value was greater than $15,000, so there would be no difficulties in borrowing that amount. There was no requirement other than a sufficient cash value to be 'approved' to borrow the cash from his own policy. He did so.

He took a tax-free loan at 4.10% from his policy, while the principal (his policy's then cash value) earned 8.40% that year. This means that he made a 4.30% positive arbitrage (gain to Jose) on money he was using for himself.

He began paying this loan (i.e.: himself) back on his own terms. Should he die before fully paying back the loan his heirs have no worries. The loan would be liquidated by the life insurance policy before paying the remainder out to his beneficiaries. Jose has continued to use the IUL loan approach for his business, made money with his tax-free loans, and has referred about 5 or 6 clients to us.

You are reading this correctly: You can borrow from yourself when you hold such a policy. You can borrow up to the cash value you have developed in the policy. You pay interest on the loan, yes, but here is another benefit that keeps your investment growing: You pay the interest to yourself, depositing it into your policy's cash value.

There is a borrow-from-yourself option with 401(k) accounts. It is not the same at all! You don't earn the interest. You cannot set the terms. If you leave the job providing the 401(k), you must immediately pay the loan back in full. Not the same at all.

When you borrow from your own IUL you are

- getting a loan from yourself
- able to borrow up to the amount of your policy's cash value
- paying interest (typically lower than market rates from a lending institution) to yourself and thereby increasing your policy cash value
- still allowing your account balance to earn interest as if you had never borrowed a dime

This last point is called positive arbitrage. Loans you have taken do not have to be repaid from your account until you pass away unless you choose to, and they are paid off by the life insurance. The only condition is that you must still have the IUL in force on the day you die.

Again, a properly structured plan is the best protection. You need to work with a trained agent or adviser who knows the rules.

Funding an IUL allows you complete control as to when you access your money: No early withdrawal penalties exist in these vehicles, unlike 401(k)s and the like. You also need not start to take forced MRD's (minimum required distributions) at age 72, something that traditional plans do require so taxes can begin to be paid weather you like it or not.

Liquidity is very important. Flexibility and funding options are likewise important. By moving your money from accounts that are 'forever taxed' to accounts that are 'never taxed', you can literally set yourself up for financial success with such a vehicle.

It is a way for you to take control of your retirement future, all your money and access to it.

The All-Important 'Living Benefits'

HAVE YOU BEEN NOTICING HOW many benefits you are 'racking up' by investing in an IUL? We are not done yet!

Another benefit of having complete control over your money is that today's IUL's come with living benefits. Most people think of an insurance policy as paying out only upon the death of the policy holder. I talk about this aspect of the vehicle as much as the money-growth and the money-protection aspects of it.

These IUL agreements allow you access to the life insurance during your lifetime.

Here is an example of how: Should you suffer a critical illness, as I illustrated with an early story, your policy can pay out cash so that you can cover your living expenses (even the medical ones) while recuperating. It is like a long-term care attached to it at no additional cost. Chronic illness, terminal illness or in some cases even a critical injury can be paid as 'living benefits.' This way you can accelerate a portion of the death benefit to cover medical bills or any exceptional expense you incur.

In a nutshell, with an IUL, you have the following benefits:

- no limitation as to how much you can contribute to an IUL
- the upside potential of the market without its downside risk
- liquidity since you may need access to the money before you retire
- ability to lend yourself your own money
- up to double digit returns in the good years (with an 8-9% average return over the past 20 years)
- your gains are locked in on a yearly basis
- should you pass away with an active policy, the entire account passes tax-free to your heirs
- you have long term care coverage in the form of living benefits

Truly Safe

ANOTHER BENEFIT OF THIS TYPE of life insurance is that in most U.S. states the money accumulated in the cash value is 'judgement protected'. This means that the money in your plan is exempt from seizure by judgment creditors. This is worth mentioning since we live in a litigation-happy society and anyone can sue you with or without cause. So, having a place to keep money out of the reach of suits is a huge benefit—and your IUL is the place.

This is the **most powerful benefit** available today in the tax code.

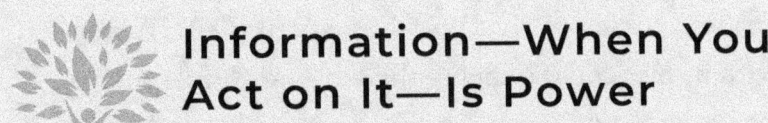

Information—When You Act on It—Is Power

THOSE FEW PROFESSIONALS AROUND ME who know about this instrument say that this is the most powerful benefit available today in the tax code.

It is all at once:

- A safe-haven for your hard-earned cash—even if you only count the principle (the actual cash you put into it) that does not lose value due to inflation
- A wealth-building tool, earning interest and profits that grow over the years you hold it
- A living benefit—a source of that cash you may need in an emergency
- A real-life insurance policy, with benefits payable upon your death to your named beneficiaries
- Tax-free money, always accessible to you without penalty
- Tax-free loans
- Tax-free inheritance

Life insurance is greatly misunderstood, and most think of it in relation to death. That is still true with the IUL but carries with it the benefit of being the most powerful source of tax-free income while you are alive and a welcomed tax-free benefit to your family when you die.

Today's IULs are more about life and living benefits than about death. They are the "Swiss knife" of life insurance and a great tool to get ahead in this complex financial world.

The sooner you begin the more you can have and the longer your income will run. You will sleep better knowing your money is protected and covered if you become ill.

Many clients have told me they wish they had known about this years ago. I just tell them to get started where they are now.

83% of Americans will *not* have enough money to get them through retirement.

I hope that you will take the time to look at the videos and the information provided here…so that you are one of the 17% who have taken care of your financial future.

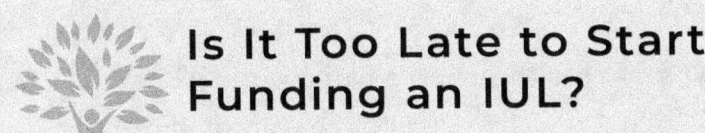

Is It Too Late to Start Funding an IUL?

YOU MIGHT BELIEVE—FROM YOUR UNDERSTANDING that an insurance policy is funded by annual premiums over 25-35 years—that you are too old to start with such an investment in your retirement. That you are too old to 'make it worth it'.

Not so! Definitely not true!

My clients range in age from 35 to 62, with an average of 45.

At age 45, you certainly have plenty of time to open, fund and watch such a policy grow before retirement in your sixties. You have 20 more years for your funded policy to gain profits and grow from compound interest. Don't wait. Do it now! The younger you start, the greater the exponential growth.

But what about those of you who are nearer to retirement? Is it too late to fund a new IUL policy at, say, age 62 or even 65, 68?

No! Again, no—it is not too late!

If you have great health, are even perhaps still working, and 'just know' that you'll enjoy 20 or more years of life—go for it. Do it now. Do it with me or another trained professional so that it is done right. But do it!

I say that even at age 65 you can benefit because the IUL honestly takes 'only' about 10 years of annual funding and patience at letting it grow in order to build a retirement income of consequence for you.

If you begin even at age 65, by 75 years of age you can take out sufficient income to 'bridge the gap', so to speak, between your Social Security benefits (and perhaps other pension monies) and your actual costs of living.

All this said, once the policy is open and you have been funding it for two years minimum, the money can be taken in the form of a loan to yourself. That is not long at all, however old you are. Two years, and you can take a loan to fund your cost of living, or a purchase such as a vehicle, or a vacation, or medical bills, or a new business startup—up to you, since it is your tax-free money.

As you might guess, your policy cash value—which is the only value that limits the amount of the loan you take—after 2 years is much less than after 5, 10 or 25 years.

Again, and this is a general observation of my clients' usage of these policies, you'll need to fund it at least 2-5 years to see your cash value amount grow to a sizeable enough value to serve you as loans.

The younger you start,
the greater the
exponential growth.

Can I Afford to Do This?

THE AVERAGE CONTRIBUTION TO THESE plans is $5,000 per year. 'Average' shows you that some clients pay in a lower annual amount than this and others more. Again, the younger you start, the greater the exponential growth.

I find that younger people don't have the future perspective they need to start right away—though it would benefit them no end to do so if only because of the effortless, safe growth of their cash outlays—and cannot really see the value of the IUL. They are still into a "retirement is so far away!" frame of mind. They so easily spend their 'extra' money raising their children, funding college and so on that retirement is the last thing they save for.

There are two typical ways of funding such policies. The first is to pay in a fixed 'premium' amount every year on the same date for 20 to 30 years. You can certainly do that if you have the years ahead of you (and at age 45, you do). The second way is good for you if you have already put a lot of cash into traditional retirement vehicles or even in a personal stock investment account. You can do what is called 'front-loading'—funding the policy in full not over 20 or 30 years but within the first 5 years.

I have clients who fund their new IUL in the amount of $25,000 per year for 5 years (because financially they can) and then stop funding it. Once the policy is fully funded, they stop paying in every year. They just let the cash value grow and grow.

Others transfer all their funds from their 'all-taxable' retirement accounts, such as 401(k) or IRA accounts, in lump sums over five years and they have fully funded their policy. Likewise, once the policy is fully funded, they stop paying in every year. They just let the cash value grow and grow. So, the taxes are paid now that they are low and spread out over 5 years to mitigate the tax liability.

Both types of clients let the policy earn profits on its investments and grow—and know that if needed, they can begin taking a regular income or just a loan out of the policy after another 5 years.

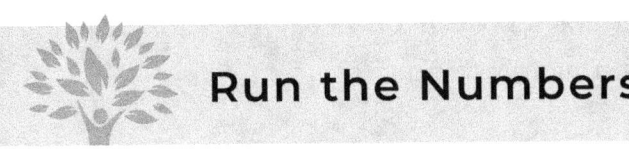

Run the Numbers

IN AN IUL INSURANCE POLICY, you are earning a 'CAGR". What is this? The CAGR interest, meaning Compound Annual Growth Rate, is the actual return on any investment. You want to know the CAGR of any and all of your investments, but frankly, most of us do not! And by the way, if you hold any retirement plan at all, you are an investor!

According to Investopedia.com, "CAGR is one of the most accurate ways to calculate and determine returns for anything that can rise or fall in value over time."

Here is why not knowing your CAGR is misleading you: Wall Street will always give you the <u>average</u> return on their various investment prospectus and performance reports. That is not going to be your CAGR reality. It is not going to be your actual or real rate of return. You know the old disclaimer "Past performance is not a guarantee of future returns"? Oh so true!

CAGR is a way to track your investments' real performance. You need to know your CAGR so that you can compare actual (not average, not estimated, but real) profits/losses of all your investment instruments.

The math you will see in the chart below is correct, but it somewhat misleads the average investor. As you can see below the (CAGR) is Zero, no gain at all. Yet, the 'average gain' shows a profit—a gain of 25%! The raw math is correct, but as you can see it is quite misleading as to the actual dollars of profit you have made.

2 Year "Average Return" According to Wall Street

YEAR

#1 $100,000 + 100% = $200,000

#2 $200,000 - 50% = $100,000

```
        100%
       - 50%
       +50%  divided by 2 years  = "Average Gain"        = 25%
       Actual rate of return "CAGR" Compound Annual Growth Rate = 0 %
```

Wall Street has been able to get away with this misrepresentation for quite some time. I just thought you should know what you are looking at when you see those numbers quarterly or annually.

Circling back to our IUL instrument: When I use a financial calculator to compare what a prospective client's investments are returning to him as profits (or losses) as opposed to what the IUL could achieve with the same starting amount of cash, the superiority of the IUL is clear to see.

The numbers show that—with a mere 6.5% conservative rate of return— the IUL will beat any retirement plan available for the same funding.

We take into consideration the tax-bracket, fees, starting age and time before beginning an income stream. The fact that taxes are eliminated and fees lowered about 30-50%, the IUL is the undisputed winner!

The spreadsheet that I produce for you—and based on your personal financial situation of earnings and savings, your current type of investments and your future retirement goals—can certainly also be evaluated by your CPA and given a 'reality check'.

Numbers don't lie! It leaves no doubt as to what a better vehicle the IUL—**the Indexed Universal Life Insurance Policy**—is for investing and saving for your working life requirements (loans) and retirement needs (income).

Learn More

I'D BE HAPPY TO SIT with you in person or get on a phone or web-based conference call to walk you through the numbers that apply to you right now. I can show you how you could benefit from contracting for an IUL Insurance Policy with all the advantages I have presented in this booklet.

 For a complimentary illustration of how an IUL could work for you, schedule a call with me here: **https://calendly.com/richardholtheuer**

 Find me on:
https://www.linkedin.com/in/holtheuer

To watch a recorded webinar on this topic, you can go to:
www.holtheuergroup.com/casestudy

 For a slightly different take on this instrument, view this video of Mr. Ed Slott on the subject the advantages of an IUL over mainstream retirement plans:

www.holtheuergroup.com/videos

What clients are saying about Richard Holtheuer and *The Smart Money Method*

"Richard has a wealth of experience in the insurance industry. He truly cares for people and will not sell you something you don't need. Instead, he will find solutions for you that you didn't even know existed. I highly recommend Richard and his services."

— **PHIL WISE,** Wise Home Inspections

"Richard looked at my retirement options and was able to make all of my options clear. He also developed a plan of action that will allow me and my wife to retire and know that we won't run out of money. He definitely helped us design our peace of mind retirement plan. Recommended him to family members and friends already. Thank you."

— **CHRIS SUAREZ,** Certified eCommerce Marketing Specialist

"Richard is a true professional. He is very knowledgeable and thorough. Richard took the time to understand my needs and then provided me with several options to ensure my financial needs were met. The ongoing communication and quality of service was top notch, and at a level rarely seen or experienced these days in the finance industry. I would recommend Richard for sound financial advice."

— **GUSTAVO A. CASTILLO,** Producing Sales Manager at Hamilton Group Funding, Inc.

"I highly recommend Richard for your retirement planning. He is a good friend and advisor. He is very professional, trustworthy and always looks out for his clients' best interests. He also helped me with my living trust and made this arduous process much easier."

— **NOULY DIMITROPOULOS,** Sales Engineer/Product Manager at Stainless Doors

"I had been highly satisfied with [Richard's] services as a financial advisor in the area of life insurance for retirement. [He] is constantly improving [his] knowledge in this theme and advising me how to proceed in the best way for my interests. In addition [he] had been very open and honest during all these 8 or more years of service to me, giving me the confidence and security on my investments with [his] recommendations!"

— **MARIA EUGENIA FUENMAYOR,** IS Project Manager

"I've known Richard for years and his knowledge for retirement planning is astonishing. The knowledge paired with his care and desire to help is what makes him the best at what he does!"

— **ANDREW ATCHINSON,** Career Agent at US Health Advisor

www.ingramcontent.com/pod-product-compliance
Lightning Source LLC
Chambersburg PA
CBHW070304220526
45465CB00004B/1745